# Slate Voices:
# Islands of Netherlorn

*for Ian*

# Mavis Gulliver

*Mavis Gulliver*

CinnamonPress

INDEPENDENT  INNOVATIVE  INTERNATIONAL

Published by Cinnamon Press
Meirion House
Glan yr afon
Tanygrisiau
Blaenau Ffestiniog
Gwynedd LL41 3SU
www.cinnamonpress.com

ISBN 978-1-909077-24-9

British Library Cataloguing in Publication Data. A CIP record for this book can be obtained from the British Library

Designed and typeset in Palatino by Cinnamon Press
Cover image: © Mavis & Richard Gulliver
Cover design by Cottia Fortune-Wood and Jan Fortune

Printed in Poland

Cinnamon Press is represented in the UK by Inpress Ltd www.inpressbooks.co.uk and in Wales by the Welsh Books Council www.cllc.org.uk.

# Acknowledgements

Some of the poems have been previously published. 'Ardencaple' appeared in *Northwords Now,* 'Imagine' in *Poetry Scotland,* 'Far North' and 'Midwinter Sun' on *Poetry Scotland's Open Mouse* and 'Toberonochy Shore' in *Southlight.*

I am indebted to the following publications and museums:
*Netherlorn, Argyllshire and its Neighbourhood,* Patrick H Gillies, first published 1909 by Virtue & Co, now available in facsimile by BiblioLife, LLC.
*The Islands that Roofed the World,* Mary Withall, Luath Press Ltd, 2001.
*Seil Island,* Michael Shaw, Eastop Publications, 2007 & 2010.
Kilchattan Kirkyard, Luing History Group, 2007.
The archives of *The Oban Times.*
The Scottish Slate Islands Heritage Trust Museum in Ellenabeich.
The Easdale Island Folk Museum.

I have great pleasure in thanking Jan Fortune for journeying with me through slate landscapes past and present. Thanks too, to everyone at Cinnamon Press for belief and encouragement, my husband Richard for travelling with me in every sense of the word, Ann Drysdale, Kevin MacNeil, Angela Skrimshire, Kenneth Steven and David Mark Williams for reading my manuscript. For a wealth of information I am grateful to The Scottish Slate Islands Heritage Trust, especially Jim Watson; the Luing History Group, especially Phil Robertson, Zoe Fleming and Norman Bissell; the Lorn Natural History Group, especially Richard Wesley, also Anni Donaldson and Innes MacLeod. A special thanks goes to the skippers and crew of ferries to Luing and Easdale and to David Ainsley of Seil Sealife Adventures for taking me to Belnahua.

# Contents

# Belnahua

# Response to Cwmorthin

In memory of the forgotten women

and the children who died before their time.

# Islands of Netherlorn

completes the circle of the half-moon arch

## Islands of Netherlorn

The islands are quiet now. Museums strive to keep memories alive, but no voice is left to tell the way it was. Yet stories speak in quarry walls, in flooded pools, in ruined powder stores, in rows of white-washed cottages, in beds of ancient slate –

fields strewn with slate, tombstones carved from slate. Slate on cottage roofs, in harbour walls, in barriers built to try to stem the sea. Beaches heaped with slate. Waves turn and toss it, shift and sculpt it, but cannot wash it away, for these are the slate islands and slate will remain.

## The approach

*'the narrowest strait I ever was in, dividing that island (Seil) from Lorn, in parts so contracted as would admit the flinging of an arch from shore to shore'*
– Thomas Pennant (1772)

Down Clachan Sound high tide runs a river. It fills the narrow channel – rushes, surges, splashes, tumbles under the hump-back bridge – creates a confusion of cross-currents, eddies and floating flecks of foam.

At low tide the flow slows, the ocean falls away – leaves rock and boulder, stone and sediment exposed. In the shallows seaweeds shift and swirl. Deep water, smooth, glass-glossed, captures clouds, scraps of sky; completes the circle of the half-moon arch.

Once folk waited for low tide, waded – or paid a penny for a ride, made the crossing on a woman's back. The bridge brought change – rumble of carts, clatter of hooves – long silences between. Now, traffic rarely stops – commuters, buses, vans; coaches pause while tourists cross on foot, take photographs, lean on the parapet, admire the view.

We stand on the hump-back, look north where contours climb, thin strips of salt marsh grade to grass, grass to bracken, bracken to birch, birch to silhouettes against the sky; look south to wider water, scattered islets, swift currents, lazy backwaters where small boats tilt and sway.

We complete the crossing – find ourselves on Seil.

We complete the crossing – find ourselves on Seil

Seil

Ellenabeich – a sea-filled shell

# Seil

By the bridge we see few signs of slate.

*Tigh an Truish* – House of Trousers – the inn where men removed
banned Highland dress, changed to trews on pain of prisonment; petrol
pumps – last chance to fill your tank. Houses line the road on either
side, gardens border shore or skirt the slopes.

Handed down and still in use today, Gaelic names are scattered on the
map. They tell of times when people knew the land – plants, animals,
history.

*Caisteal Acha Luachrach* – Castle of the Field of Rushes
*Puilladobhran* – Pool of the Otter
*Port nam Faoileann* – Port of the Seagulls
*Rubha nan Ròn* – Skerry of the Seals
*Sloc nan Sgarbh* – Gully of the Cormorant
*Cnoc an Tighe Mhòir* – The Hill of the Great House
*Dun Mucaig* – Fortress of the Boar
*Rudha na Garbhairde* – The Promontory of the Rough Heights

Footpaths lead through woods of oak and ash to moorland, cliff and
shore – stony bays, raised beaches, dykes and stacks, folded strata –
dips and anticlines, valley bogs, dimpled hills, rocky outcrops poking
through the sward; sea loch havens – anchorage for yachts, haunts of
otter, heron, mallard, teal; bands of slate that tempted men to break and
scar the land.

The road curves with the coast – south to Balvicar's shop, flooded
quarry, golf course, boatyard, pier; new houses cluster round the Bay,
spill into fields, outnumber quarriers' cottages. On to North Cuan –
ferry port for Luing; or west to Smiddy Brow where islands lie below
us like a map – sea stretching away to Scarba, Islay, Jura, Colonsay.

We come again at night – distances disappear in moonless, starless
dark. Cottage windows glow, pinpoint villages, Ellenabeich, Easdale,
Cullipool on Luing. Fladda's lighthouse warns of skerries, reefs, Grey
Dog's tidal race.

No light shows where Belnahua lies.

## Beginning and End

silt and mud compressed
in shallow seas, heated
to blue-black sheets of rippled slate;

broken, blasted,
thrown to disarray
by centuries of toil and quarrying.

but like the moon
the slate trade
waxed and waned,

so many reasons
leading to demise;
quarries worked out,

the flood of '81,
outbreak of war,
roof tiles made of clay,

Welsh slate –
mines like Cwmorthin
hastening the end.

# Ardencaple

Abandoned long ago,
and poached for stone,
only low walls remain –
each crevice home to spleenwort,
wall rue, moss,
each family's space so small
a rowan's branches stretch
from wall to wall.

Small quarries where they worked
are overgrown.
From slate-strewn floors
and leaf-clogged pools
trees strain to reach the light,
cast shade on man-made cliffs,
slimed walls that drip and trickle
when it rains.

# Far North

We reach Seil's north-east tip,
stand by the cleft
that lets the ocean through,
mainland Argyll
a river width
away.

A windless day
when slack tide holds
its breath,
seaweeds rest,
small fish leap,
leave tiny splashes –
rings that widen
fade.

Herons stand knee deep
or rise protesting,
settle in the trees,
or land
on ancient waste banks,
lose themselves
as grey-black plumage
merges
with grey slate.

## Midwinter Sun

Walk south
along Seil's coast to Cuan Sound
and shield your eyes

for low sun turns all water into gold,
to shimmering light
that dazzles, dazzles.

Sea between islands, rock pools,
turning waves, marshy hollows,
dew damp scraps of slate,

dripping cliffs, small waterfalls,
burns that thread the hill land to the sea,
each one reflects and magnifies the light.

And wigeon, when they rise
send showers of twinkling droplets
from their wings.

# Lagoon

Sea sorts the slate –
sifts and grades
makes banks and ridges,
platforms, slanting slopes,
builds a wall
to mark the last high tide
where every slate slots in.

Another day –
another tide
the view is not the same.
The sea has been at work.
What it makes it breaks
what it brings
it takes away again.

Only the pool
behind the bank remains,
sea water seeps
through gaps between the slate,
leaves a lagoon
that's smoother
than the sea.

# Ellenabeich

Eilean a-beithich,
      Isle of Birches
stripped by quarrymen,
plundered by ocean.

All that remains,
      a sea-filled shell,
slate shipped out, waste tipped
        to fill the narrow channel,
add new land to Seil.

A village
built on top of shattered spoil,
      Ellenabeich –
named for a land that's gone.

Homes for men
who worked to win the slate,
families crowded
      into two small rooms.

Sea bed buried under cottages,
narrow streets,
      walled garths,
        broken slate.

# Going to Church

*'the vast fleet of slate-makers' boats from the islands, crowded with men, women and children, coming to attend church ... floating on the raging tide... no return being possible until the ebbing waters had come back exhausted, and until, changing their course, they had come back in full flood to carry home*
                                    — Alexander Beith (*A Highland Tour*, 1845)


Six days they laboured.
On the seventh – no hope of rest –
when tides were right they clambered into boats,
rowed with the flow along the Cuan Sound,
worshipped,
waited
            for turn of tide
                        to help them home.


When seas were rough they walked.

We followed in their footsteps,
skirted shore,
climbed up and over moor
where rain flew in
            like needles on the wind,

imagined them, inadequately clad,
arriving drenched,
            feet sodden,
                        shivering,
cold  s e e p i n g
            through psalms,
                        sermon,
                              prayers –
the  l o n g
            walk back.

## Wild Weather

Life on the western edge
inures you to gales
so that sometimes you sleep
through them,

unaware, until morning
of missing roof tiles,
battered blooms, shattered
greenhouse glass.

Did they in eighteen-eighty-one
hear the ocean's roar,
see the tidal wave
that drowned their world?

Or did they sleep to wake
wide-eyed, incredulous,
their quarry swamped,
two-hundred feet
of hollowed ground
brim-filled with ocean?

## Storm at Ellenabeich

Shags seek shelter from the open sea
where white waves thunder
menacing and high.

Inside the quarry's flood
they ride tossed water,
dive, disappear...

Sea pours through gaps,
tops rocks,
runs down in waterfalls...

Easdale disappears
in slanting rain.
The old pier fades.

No-one walks the streets.
Only shags bob up
and dive again.

# Easdale

an open boat, a narrow stretch of sea

# Easdale

*'quherein ther is abundance of skalzie (slate) to be win'*
– Dean Munro (fl. 1526- 1574)

Viewed from Ellenabeich, houses crowd Easdale's eastern end. Wall meets wall, roof touches roof, rows of chimneys sprout above grey slate. The whinstone dyke stands dark above them all, its outline cast against the bulk of Mull.

The 'Fladda' waits to ferry us across – an open boat, a narrow stretch of sea. No charge is made for outward trips. We could stay for ever, never pay the fare. Four hundred feet of sea, three minutes and we're there; yet when gales blow, sea storms down Easdale Sound, boats are hauled up, people stranded.

We land on a different world. There is no road. Transport is by wheelbarrow – rusting metal, home-made out of wood, cottage numbers painted on their sides. They stand by the slipway – wait to carry shopping home. The only vehicles dredge the harbour, an endless task of shifting slate that slips from spoil heaps, swirls in on the tide. The harbour cuts deep into the island. Terraced cottages, wide grassed squares, alleys, steps, bramble-tangled garths, flooded quarries, tons of surplus slate fill the few windswept acres.

No-one needs to live here now. Quarrying ended, families left, few remained to see the slow decay. Others came from choice – charmed by peace, clean air, views that change as often as the weather. Gales can blow in summer, winters can be mild, seasons mingle – still they come and go.

In springtime, blackthorn buds break into bloom, a song thrush carols from a chimney top. Summer fills cottages; swallows dip and skim the quarry pools, air hums to buzz of bees, shimmers above sun-baked slate. Dawn comes early, dusk falls late. Days are long.

Autumn ripens blackberry and sloe. Swallow and wheatear leave. Holiday homes are boarded up and locked. Residents prepare for winter, secure boats, bins, garden gates. Smoke curls from chimney pots, is carried on the wind, or hangs on air when days are calm and still. Dawn comes late, dusk falls early. Nights are long.

# First Visit

Even on a sun-silvered day,
when this waste of slate
is dotted with heather
and cliffs are green with ivy,
there is melancholy here.
It floods my mind
the way the sea once topped
the quarry walls.

It tells of men who slaved
to split the slate,
women and children,
backs bent under waste,
trudging tracks
to tip it in the sea;
of wet winds blowing,
blowing from the west.

# Early Quarrying

*From an article in* The Miners Journal *February 1864 by John White, manager of the Easdale Slate Company.*

before they learned to blast
whole families tuned their lives
to wind
to waves
to rhythm of the sea

children
searched for sea-split slates
carried them
beyond the pull of tide

women
stacked larger slates in creels
for endless
back-bent trekking
up the shore

men
worked the lowest reaches
of the beach
toiled longest at spring tides
came to understand
the strata's slope   skew cuts
slip joints   cleavage seams
drove seasoned hardwood wedges
into cracks
waited
for tide on tide to swell the wood
drove wedges deeper
waited
for cracks to widen
force the blocks apart
hand barrowed them
above high water mark

day or night
they raced the ebb and flow
stripped the shore
reduced the island's boundary with the sea

# The Night of 21-22 November, 1881

*An Easdale woman relates her experience of the storm. Details for this imagined account are taken from* The Oban Times *and* The Oban Telegraph.

I'll try my best to tell you how it was
but words can't show the terror of that night.
As water rose my faith near ebbed away –
I saw the awful way our lives would end,
torn from our loved ones, screaming in the sea,
our bodies cast up on some distant shore
or lost for ever, carried on the tide,
denied the peace of consecrated ground.

Praise God he spared us, not a soul was lost.
Some bless the quarries – say they broke the force,
swallowed the ocean's strength and saved our lives.
And that seems just for we would not be here
without the quarries and the work they bring.

I'll tell you this – that night has changed us all,
my glance is always straying to the sea.
Look at it now, so calm you'd scarce believe
the way it raced and roared and filled our homes.
I cannot trust the ebb and flow of tides
nor can I rest. My nights are filled with fear
and if I sleep my dreams are filled with sea.

And how can I give comfort to my bairns
when I can't promise sea won't rise again?
They scream at night, afraid to go to bed,
and where they once played happy on the shore
they cling around my skirts and stay inside.

We knew the wind was rising. All the men
had left the quarry, hauled up all the boats
or tied the ones too heavy to be moved,
then to our beds, secure against the storm
                              – or so we thought,

but sea and wind grew louder, noise enough
to rouse the dead – roaring, whining, whistling
through the chinks until our heads were filled
with nothing else –
                              and still it rose.

The door burst open, sea came roaring in
as if the Lord had sent another flood.
It swept us from the box bed, threw me down,
I struggled, choking, coughing up the sea,
and reached the ladder. How? I cannot tell
but clambered up to soothe my frightened bairns.

The water followed, swirled around our heels.
We clung together while it rose and rose.
We pierced the roof and crawled up to the ridge,
held tight the bairns and hoped to storm it out,
huddled in darkness, feared the water's rise,
waited for daybreak, prayed the tide would turn.

Others, we learned had tried to reach the hill,
but water's force had swept them off their feet
so neighbours took them in and there we sat
perched on the rooftops like a flock of birds.
We prayed, sang psalms to keep our spirits up
to no avail –
                              for still the water rose...

At last, at dawn the tide began to ebb
and such a cheer rang out from every roof,
our lives were saved –
                              but then we saw the loss.

The pier had swept away, and sea had claimed
the stacks of slates that waited to be shipped.
With luck we'll find some when the tides are low
but like as not they'll all be smashed to bits
and double work will not mean double pay.

There's water everywhere – but none to drink.
The pipes from Seil were smashed beneath the sea,
and water butts are tainted with the salt.

Walls breached and quarries filled up to the brim,
tools gone – submerged or carried far away,
the livestock taken – cattle, chickens, pigs,
our boats all shattered, broken, lost at sea -
the things that take a lifetime to collect...
and how can we buy more – always in debt –
lives 'on the slate' one pay day to the next
for on that day there's nothing left to spare.

Look at us now, my man needs boots for work,
the bairns and I go barefoot – not a shoe
between us. We're used to that in summer
but there are months of winter yet to come.
Lord Breadalbane has promised all he can
but what can one man do – for all his wealth,
and even he can't take the fear away.

The tide went out, the water level fell,
drained from the loft space, poured out through the door,
took with it almost everything we owned –
dishes and pans, the scuttle full of coal,
potatoes that we'd grown, our sack of oats,
and things I knew we never could replace.
The Holy Bible father handed down,
a record of our family's names and dates –
and all it left was sodden, filthy, spoiled,
no kindling dry enough to light a fire,
no garments to replace our soaking clothes.

They say the waves rushed in at three o'clock
and that at six , the tide began to ebb,
but in my mind it lasted all night long.
We searched the hill, the alleys and the green
for something that would ease the awful loss,
but it was hopeless.

       Pray forgive me, Sir,
for we are left in such a sorry state
I choke on words and cannot tell you more.

# The Last Duchess, 1902

*Lucrezia, wife of Alfonso, Duke of Ferrara was immortalised in Browning's poem 'The Last Duchess.'*
*The slates were given names according to their size. Duchess, at 24" x 12" was the second largest. The last Duchess, quarried on Easdale in 1902, can be seen in The Scottish Slate Islands Heritage Trust Museum in Ellenabeich.*

Not Lucrezia,
whose smiles stopped altogether
at the Duke's command –
but the last slice of slate,
split from quarried rock,
trimmed to Duchess size,
reminder of an industry's demise,
memorial
to those who spent their lives
on these small islands
quarrying the slate.

# The Naming of Slates

If I was a child
I'd want to jump the rope
to chanted names.

*Princess, Duchess, Countess, Ladies,*
*Headers, Doubles, Sizeable, Undersize.*

I'd want to feel the rhythm
in my feet, the swing of rope –
turning, turning.

*Princess, Duchess, Countess, Ladies,*
*Headers, Doubles, Sizeable, Undersize.*

I like to think the girls
had time to skip, arms windmilling,
the frayed rope hissing,

*Princess, Duchess, Countess, Ladies,*
*Headers, Doubles, Sizeable, Undersize.*

bare feet leaping, landing, leaping,
a joyful game, a break
from hauling slate.

*Princess, Duchess, Countess, Ladies,*
*Headers, Doubles, Sizeable, Undersize.*

But was there space to swing a rope –
and were the names of slates
best left unsung?

# Aspirations

As lads we played at blasts,
watched quarrymen
reducing rock to rubble,
blowing cliffs apart –
wanted to be them,
not splitters and dressers
waiting for blocks of slate
to come to us.

We wanted to hang from ropes,
bore holes, pack powder,
light the fuse,
give warning shouts,
run for our lives
to hide while slabs broke loose
and fragments flew
to splatter in the sea.

Few of us made it,
most were labourers,
some, apprenticed,
learned to split and dress,
five years to learn a trade
that paid a pittance
for a hundred slates.

## Imagine

I cannot grasp
what lies beneath these pools:
how five million slates a year
and all this spoil
could be man-handled
from the depths of one small isle.
I close my eyes,
imagine above the gull's scream,
the rhythmic thud of pumps,
warning shouts, gunpowder blast,
ring of iron, break of slate,
men coughing,
clearing lungs of dust,
black spit sizzling on sun-hot waste
or caught by wild winds –
flying out of sight.

## The Swimming Quarry

On this rare day
            the quarry pool is smooth
as polished rock,
sun and cloudless sky combine
to hint
            at what the depth of water holds.

A scum of floating algae draws a line
where water stops
                        meets rock,
above its mark – bare walls,
below – cushioned algae, thick as winter fur
green that fades
            and falls
                        to murky depths.

A dyke – a towering bulk
                        of unworked rock
bisects the quarry's width,
a blue-grey shape, dark near the surface
            shades to palest blue
                        as if its colour bled.

Youngsters dive
            or leap from quarry top,
tread water
            next to ledges where men worked
swim
            through spaces
                        emptied
                                    of their slate.

## Easdale Exodus

Not the procession of people
leaving the small island,
the lost livelihood,
but a ripple of tiny toads
leaving the flooded quarries.

Masters of a toad triathlon
they swim in perfect symmetry of style,
leap, a long jump feat
five times their single centimetre length,
crawl, a slow laborious heaving
up shards of shattered slate
as they cross the no-man's land
between water and the refuge
of grass, wood sage and heather.

They too face uncertainty,
playthings for cats,
morsels for hooded crows,
the lightning stab of heron's bill.

Some will survive,
return to pools,
an annual migration
like summer people
clinging to family histories,
returning to roots
in rows
of whitewashed cottages.

## Remnants

The industry has gone
but slate still dominates.
Eyes can't escape
the endless stretch of waste
that failed to cleave.
Piled in heaps it litters land
and slips
       beneath the sea.

Ears can't escape
the crunch on well worn paths,
chink as thin slates snap,
clatter of unstable scree,
thunder rumble on the shore
when slate is turned and tumbled
and the backwash
       drags and rolls.

slate still dominates

# Leaving Easdale

We walk around the island one last time, cross the harbour while the
tide is low, avoiding ropes and chains that anchor boats, past cottages,
heaps of wasted slate, a powder store that's empty, roofless now; find a
place where slates were split and shaped, half-hidden hollows lined
with dry-slate walls – supporting posts and canvas roofs all gone.

We cross the 'causeway', bridge of un-worked rock, quarries filled with
water on each side – *Creag a monadh* – quarry of the hill, *Creag na uam* –
quarry of the cave. Up the slope along the quarry edge, past broken
buildings – forge and engine-house, boiler-house where lifting gear
was powered; three flooded quarries on the western side, the
southernmost with curving concrete wall.

A kestrel hovers high above the hill and all along the path are
celandines. We leave the wilderness of broken garths, discarded slate
half-hid in undergrowth, coupling of toads within Whyte's Well,
blackbirds nesting in a bramble patch; cross to quarries East and West;
return to close-mown paths, cottages around the grassy square, hall,
museum, restaurant, waiting room.

The ferry brings the children home from school – lifejackets orange,
bright against the sea. Dogs wait to greet them, shouts and laughter
travel up the brae.

We board, head into waves that spray our lips with salt, pass steamer
pier remains, a timbered bulk no longer joined to land. We pay the fare,
step ashore on Seil, tread paths to grass-topped cliffs where jackdaws,
ravens, buzzards claim the sky.

Look down from Dun Mor's height, see Easdale as a model of itself.
Houses, boats, people, the wave-washed fringe of slate around the
shore, gabions, spurs of un-worked rock, quarries filled with sky, the
whinstone ridge, harbour wall, heaps of wasted slate – all made
miniature.

Yet sounds are magnified – a dog's bark, children's laughter,
intermittent crowing of a cock; the chug of the ferry making the
crossing   over   and over.

sheltering on the leeward side

Luing

Cullipool – coastline gnawed by quarrying and sea

# Luing

*Ane ile callit Luying…with ane paroche kirk, gude name land inhabit and maurite…
having sufficient for highland galies in it…*

– Dean Munro (fl.1526-1574)

(An isle called Luing, with one parish church, good land inhabited and
manured… having sufficient (harbour) for Highland galleys in it.)

The 'Belnahua' crosses Cuan Sound. Cars drive up the slipway onto
Seil. We board – five cars, three men on foot, one dog — packed tight as
limpets in a crack. The ramp clangs, drags, scrapes, lifts. Three minutes
later we arrive on Luing.

We sit awhile, look back at ever-changing water. Close to shore the
current dawdles east, the centre rushes west, a treacherous eight knot
rip, moving mosaic of ruffles, glass-smooth swirls, breaking waves.

A shag caught in the flow, speeds past, is lost in wild water at the
Sound's mouth.

Six miles by two, the island road runs south, two ridges with a narrow
glen between, hill forts that show an early use of slate – cup-marked
doorposts, chambered walls and steps, vantage points with views for
miles around.

One church, one school, one shop, a roofless mill with waterwheel
intact, a burial ground with gravestones mainly slate, fertile pasture,
herds of cattle, sheep; roadside banks with primroses in spring,
barnacle geese that graze on winter grass.

Out west, the largest village, Cullipool; houses old and new, coastline
gnawed by quarrying and sea; beach an endless shift of broken slate.
Blackmill Bay, where steamers brought in mail, island cattle left for
Oban's mart; a link to Crinan, Glasgow and beyond.

East lies Toberonochy, its quarry flooded, bordered now with trees; two
sturdy piers, fine anchorage for boats, beach ground down to tiny
flakes of slate.

The road ends here, but Luing goes on, two miles before we reach the
southern tip.

## Port Mary

No whitewashed terraces.

The only rows
are grass-topped lines –

       embankments
built for hauling spoil away.

They lead from workings,
stretch towards the sea

like fingers
       reaching
from the quarry's hand.

# Great Mullein, Cullipool Quarry

*Verbascum thapsus has a variety of English names. Mullein, derived from the Latin*
*'mollis' refers to the softness of the leaves. Among other names honouring this quality*
*are Adam's Flannel and Cuddy Lugs. Aaron's rod refers to the rod which 'brought forth*
*buds and blossoms' (Numbers xvii.8). Candela regia comes from the practice of dipping*
*the stems in fat to make candles. Other names relating to this use are King's Taper and*
*Virgin Mary's Candle.*

Few plants thrive on this quarry floor
the soil too sparse
the shattered slate too deep.

Only Mullein reaches any height
Aaron's rod aiming for the sky
a single finger pointing at the sun.

*Candela regia* of the Romans
clustered buds and yellow flowers,
bright candles tapering.

I look into each open throat,
see tiny stamens, orange-tipped,
flames within a flower.

# Cullipool Quarry, 1938

*As seen in the British Pathé Newsreel.*

The cut-glass English accent
grates – replaces
Scottish voices, sounds of slate,
explosion's blast
with facts inaccurate.


Attempted jokes of Scottish cats
on Scottish tiles misfire,
trivialise the danger and the dirt.


I turn sound down
watch pictures flickering –
dark cliffs, the Sound beyond,
Belnahua black,
Fladda's lighthouse white.

*cut*


a quarryman suspended from two ropes
a dizzy drop below
a near-sheer face above
the rhythmic riving of the hole
packing of powder

*cut*


the blast – a cloud of dust
that rises high
to slowly dissipate
as slabs slide
down

*cut*

splitter and trimmer seated
on waste slate
chisel and mallet splitting  –
knife and block
trimming slates to size

*cut*


labourers – a chain of eight
passing slates to where
the bogey waits –
the last man stacks

*cut*


two men push the bogey on its rails
a slight incline
until the slope slips down
to Cullipool
they jump aboard –
ride towards the pier

*CUT*

## Cullipool Quarry, 2012

No flooding here,
no standing on the brink
to wonder
what the depth of water hides.
No need to imagine strata,
break of boulder, ledges,
colour of rock.

Light floods down,
accentuates them all,
reveals a score
of subtle shades of grey,
iron stains of rusted brown,
shot holes drilled to blast,
fool's gold glistening.

Nothing much grows –
a trailing bramble,
bonsai holly bush
and silence.
But tap two slates together –
they ring like bells, echoes
bouncing back
        like memories.

## Toberonochy Quarry, 2012

Behind the shore,
the well-kept cottages
and single track
the pumping house lies silent
under ivy.

Deep beneath trees
sheer cliffs
and slopes of slate,
reflected images
show perfect symmetry.

Rock reaches rock,
trunk touches trunk –
it's hard to know
where water starts
and ends.

I cast a scrap of slate
to learn the truth –
watch ripples spread,
concentric circles
reach to every edge –

transform reflections
into crizzled lines.

## Toberonochy Shore

Old photos show
the shelters by the shore,
a sloping roof, three sides,
the fourth one open,
letting in the light –
the wind and rain.

Side by side the banks-men sat,
the splitter split,
the trimmer trimmed to size,
each dependent on the other's skill
a pair could turn
a thousand slates a day.

The track that brought the blocks
is deep in trees,
its puddle floor is wet
with sodden leaves,
all trace of rails and bogeys
disappeared.

Only waste slate remains,
heaps still bare,
hollows patched with grass.
The only paths
are well-worn tracks
showing that otters now
outnumber men.

The sea is quiet, weather mild,
an ideal day to sit and split the slate;
but I'm the only person on the shore.
The village street is empty.
The loudest sound
a flight of winter geese
calling from straggled v-shapes
overhead.

# Meeting Phil Robertson at Toberonochy in 2012

We walk the quiet streets,
speak to the few we meet,
incomers,
owners of second homes,
one who moors his yacht,
explores the open sea,
makes a landfall
when it suits his mood.

No-one recalls the past
except for Phil
who came in nineteen sixty one –
not from some distant place,
but down the road from Cullipool.

We find him in a garden
brimmed with flowers –
dahlias, sweet peas, marigolds,
clematis and roses on the fence.

He takes us round the village,
shows us the window
where the men were paid,
the smithy –
now a garden shed,
engine house, the pier
where slates were shipped.

He tells of bygone times,
regretful
that his mother's native tongue
was banned in school
and not passed down to him.

He talks of bustling streets,
crowded cottages,
of how the village lost its heart
when families locked their doors
and moved away.

## Blackmill Bay

Dusk is falling fast on Blackmill Bay.
A south wind stirs dried thistle heads,
scuds clouds towards the hazy hills of Mull.

Across the water Lunga's features freeze
to jagged outlines dark against the sky.
Nothing arrives and nothing leaves the pier.

No slate is shipped, no steamers call,
no mail arrives, no puffers carry coal,
no cattle go from here to Oban's mart.

Fence posts, bent and twisted mark the edge,
holes that once held rails
are tiny windows opening onto sea.

Grass grows down the centre,
sprouts through cracks,
                              a six foot drop –

the rest is washed away,
gone with the tide or shattered
on the shore.

Sea swirls round rotting stanchions –
blackened stumps that fade in fading light,
merge with sea beneath and hills beyond.

## Ticket Office, Blackmill Bay

No tickets now,
just gulls and starlings
perching on the roof,
sheep avoiding heat
asleep in sharp-edged shadows,
rubbing against corners
to ease the itch of lice,
or sheltering
on the leeward side
when gales
tear down the Sound.

Ropes
tied to concrete blocks
old bricks
and lumps of slate
hold down the roof,
too late
to save the gables
where rain drips in,
slate and mortar slip,
and shallow-rooted dockens
wilt in August sun.

The door is padlocked
but there's life inside,
nestlings call for food,
keep up a constant chirping
that magnifies
as swallows swoop,
flit in – flit out again
while butterflies
fluttering
between curtain and glass,
find no escape.

I saw the words. I read them all – and wept.

Belnahua

each roofless room is open to the sky

# Belnahua

*'ane iyllane quharin there is fair skailzie aneuche'*

— Dean Munro (fl.1526-1574)

(An island wherein there is good slate enough.)

Twenty-seven acres set in sea – no water source, a hump of whinstone
rising seventy feet, the rest so low that nothing stays the wind. Waves
and salt spray saturate the grass.

Owners came for gain. Nothing else would bring them to this place.
They did not stay, brought others in to strip and ship the slate.

Men came for work, women and children followed – had no choice.

I read the Census – eighteen sixty-one. Queen Victoria on the throne,
newly widowed, clothed in black and jet; America in throes of Civil
War; Belnahua busy at the slate.

Two tacksmen oversee the quarry work, brothers John and Hugh, their
surname Shaw; quarrymen – twenty-six – blasting, breaking, splitting,
shaping slate; five labourers fetch and carry, haul away the waste; two
man the engines; a single smith keeps the tools in trim; two carpenters
make and mend the boats; four fishermen keep the bellies filled; two
seamen home from working on the ships; one teacher for a class of
twenty-three; one pauper now unfit for quarry work. When boats come
in they gather at the pier; unload the coal, potatoes, sacks of meal,
barrels of water from the spring on Luing; load slates for places far
away, for castles, houses, Glasgow tenements – long-lasting roofs as
barriers to rain.

Women to make life easier for men; twenty wives to cook, to clean and
mend, tend twenty seven bairns not yet in school; twelve domestic
servants helping out – spinsters and girls too young by far to wed;
Catherine May, eleven years old, maintains a house for two unmarried
men; three reduced to parish pauper state.

No doctor, nurse or midwife; no church, no minister or burial place.
When a life had ended, young or old, men rowed across two miles of
open sea, carried the body up Luing's coffin road, laid it to rest in
consecrated ground – hemmed in, weighed down by slate.

## Belnahua Beckons

i

No one will take me to Belnahua.
They say the landing is dangerous.
I would have to leap from the boat's bow–
a risk too great for them to take.
They ask why I want to land
when there's nothing there,
no road, no shop, no cars,
no homely hearth,
no women, no men, no children,
no water fit to drink.

I sit on Luing's shore,
view the dark outline,
slate beach silvered in the sun,
topping of bleached green turf.
I focus on gable ends,
holes where windows used to be,
chimneys that know no smoke,
doorways open to nothing
but sky and sea.

I imagine the exodus,
the slate trade falling off,
men answering Kitchener's call,
exchanging quarries for trenches,
eager for adventure –
the glory of war.
Women and children left
to man the pumps
until, defeated by water
they abandoned homes,
a way of life,
                    the island.

ii

Back home, I search the web,
find photographs frozen in time,
a video seen as a dream,
or as a ghost, floating
on someone else's footsteps.

Through his lens I see the smallness,
the heart of the island eaten out,
ragwort and grass as lush
inside the roofless cottages
as out around the flooded pools.

It's not enough. I sense the desolation
but need to feel the slip of slate
beneath my feet, the sea breeze
cooling on my cheek, hear waves breaking
on the fractured shore.


iii

Six months on, a chance encounter
and I'm on my way.
Outside the cottage
trees heave like rough seas
but Clachan Sound is calm,
herons stand along the shore,
an otter pops up, dives and disappears.

We leave the shelter, feel the swell,
the growing turbulence.
I'd never seen a river in the sea,
water riding water, smooth dark currents
pushing waves aside
to rear up skerries – splinter
into whirlpools – waterfalls.

The island's flat black outline comes to life.
Space grows between the cottage rows
and doorways show
the rooms that hide inside.
Each slate takes shape –
walls a neat mosaic,
shore a random patterning.

The pier has gone,
all that remains
a ridge of jutting stones
as useless as a row of rotten teeth,
the seabed moves,
its depth of shifting slate
provides no anchorage.

The skipper waits offshore.
The dinghy fights the tide,
the current's flow,
to run aground on banks
of submerged slate.
I wade through breaking waves
to reach the land.

The beach is steep,
a stretch where sea holds sway,
each slate a servant to the changing tide
each tumbled piece lies bare,
its surface smoothed;
only a rusting boiler shelters growth –
grass tussocks and a single ragwort flower.

Above the shore
grass grows so deep
I feel no slate beneath my feet.
It reaches quarries' watery rims,
clothes slopes, tops walls and gable ends,
carpets cottages, fills hearths
and window sills.

Stunted elders
shelter behind walls,
outcropped rock bears heather,
lichens, moss; but mostly there is grass,
its salt-scorched tussocked cushioning
leans to the east, covers the slate
greens the grey.

Water fills the quarries,
drowns them deep,
each surface satin smooth,
each edge reveals a downward slope of slate
until a breeze sends ripples ruffling,
obscures the view
of all that lies beneath.

Above the shore, around each quarry's edge,
buildings dot the landscape,
each roofless room is open to the sky,
no doors are left to close against the wind,
only the walls remain – bare slate,
cracked harling, doorways edged in brick,
chimneys and gables crumbling.

Machines abandoned, left to rust,
still keep their shape.
Boilers, pulleys, pistons, rods and rails
now poke through grass.
An engine stands with cogs and wheels intact.
The crane has fallen, timbers grey with age
outlive the men.

## Catherine McPhail, Remembering 1840

I wrapped her in my shawl – my Sunday best,
no matter that I'll miss it when the wind
blows from the North with ice upon its breath.

I could not bear to cover up her face.
I held her tight and rocked her in my arms
and must have fainted then, for when I woke

she'd gone. *Janet.* I know I screamed her name,
not just my voice, but every part of me
called out and willed her back, alive and well.

I had to follow. Women held me back.
I struggled, fought them off, ran to the pier
to find the boat had left. My child had gone.

I could not see for tears but heard the plash
of oars grow faint, grow faint, grow fainter yet
until the sea had swallowed up the sound.

Imagined then, the things I'd never seen,
the jetty where they'd land, the coffin road.
the kirkyard and the lair. I could not bear

to think on that – her lying there alone.
I fell down on the slate, the cold, hard slate
and prayed and waited for my man's return.

He told me how he'd laid her in the lair,
and how he'd get a gravestone with her name
so her young life would never be forgot.

Now water lies between us, thoughts may cross
but all my words are scattered by the wind.
So here I sit on Belnahua's shore,

my eyes on Luing, my thoughts all filled with her.
He took me once, to show me where she lay,
to see the slate that marked her grave and name.

I saw the words. I read them all – and wept.

ERECTED

By..

John McPhail.

Belnahuay.

To. The. Memory.

of. His. Daughter:

Janet. Who. Depar

ted Thus. Life. SEP22

AGED. 8.YEAR MDCCCXL


What of me?
She was *my* daughter too –
This gravestone bears *his* name
alongside hers
as if he was the only one who cared.
*I* was the one who bore her, felt the pain.
*I* was the one who nursed her at my breast.
Why is *my* name not written
on her grave?

*I* was the one
who weaned her, sang her lullabies,
washed and clothed her,
brushed the slate dust from her hair,
soothed bruises, dressed cut knees
and watched her grow.
*I* was the one who held her hand,
took pride in all she learned –
first tooth, first step, first word,
each one a hurdle that we had to win.

I know that children die
but this... this was cruel.
Those early days
that claim so many bairns had passed.
I thought...I dared to hope...
She was the best of my life's work.
Now she lies beneath a slab of slate
nothing is left to show I ever lived.
My child lies there and I'll lie
who knows where?

# Searching for Janet

*'Kilchattan Kirkyard' Luing History Group, 2007, gives transcripts of gravestones recorded in 2003-4. Janet's grave is number 5 in Row 3m, and described as 'Good quality flat slate, tilted, buried under turf.'*

*Janet's Birth Certificate records –*
*Janet MacPhail. Lawful daughter of John Macphail Belnahuay & his spouse Cath.*
*McPhail born 18<sup>th</sup> September 1832.*
*I have been unable to trace her Death Certificate.*


I tread between lean and list
of weathered slate,
gravestones scabbed and scarred
with lichen growth, circles and rings

of yellow, orange, brown,
blue-grey tufts,
white crusted sheets that cover
numbers, letters, words.

I reach the place
where Janet's body lies,
but grass has claimed her space,
my fingers pushed into the turf
can find no stone.

I prod the earth, listen
for metal spike to chink on rock,
expect a tiny stone to suit a child,
find instead
a six foot slab of slate.

And when the sod is lifted,
turned aside,
see that roots have filled
each letter's groove
with mirror writing,
pale as if it's bleached.

I brush away loose soil,
pebbles, a piece of glass,
find fool's gold glinting
in between the words;
reveal, not weathered text,
but incised letters, clean cut,
sharp and clear as on the day
the mason fashioned them;

gently replace the turf,
fescue and holcus,
winter leaves of flowers
yet to come –

daisy, clover, yarrow,
lady's smock.

## Matilda McLachlan 1881

*In the 1881 Census, Matilda McLachlan appears as an '80' year old pauper living alone in a one-roomed cottage. In the first Census of 1841 she lived with her husband Peter and her son, Thomas. The last record for Thomas is in 1851. Peter died of 'old age' in 1875 and Matilda of 'senile decay' in 1887. Her death certificate records her age as 100, but previous Censuses indicate that she was between 71 and 87. None of their names appear on Kilchattan gravestones. Matilda's father, Alexander Stevenson, was a Quarry Manager, so it is conceivable that Matilda spent her entire life on Belnahua.*

No joy in growing old
and that's the truth of it.
Eighty summers,
aye, and winters too.
Outlived them all,
my man, my bonnie bairns.
My sight is failing,
all I see is past.
My twisted hands
no longer wield a broom.
I cannot wring my clothes,
wash when I can,
but oh! the cold.
If I undress
I'm like to catch my death
and so I wear the same
both day and night.
I smell, I know I smell
like rotten fish.
My house smells too.
I cannot clean
the way I used to do.
My knees won't kneel,
my back's too sore to bend
and so I sit
beside a meagre fire,
wait for handouts,
neighbour's charity
and death.
It can't be long,
and truth to tell
I'm ready for the end –
for if God wills
I'll see my bairns again.

# Christina MacDonald, 1881

*Christina MacDonald from South Uist appeared in the 1881 Census as a domestic servant employed by Angus Shaw, Belnahua Quarry Master, to keep house for him and his 19 year old son.*

I had to come to work and earn my keep
to serve the Quarry Master and his son,
with no-one left at home I had no choice.
My tasks are much the same, to cook and clean,
but there are stairs, and windows made of glass,
bedrooms with hearths – a fire in every one
a luxury that I can scarce believe,
and I must carry coal and tend them all.
The house is warm. I've food enough to eat,
but all day I'm alone, and how I miss
those early days at home, the company –
my mother, brother, sisters, most of all
the wee one always asking what and why.
Instead of chatter, endless thud of pumps,
harsh warning shouts that make me catch my breath
and dread the worst until the blast has passed.
I hear the crack and fall of broken rock.
I feel the slate floor shake beneath my feet
and fear, one day, the isle will split in two
and Belnahua sink beneath the waves.
I steal a moment, stand beside the door,
longing for springs of water, fresh and sweet,
South Uist breezes, white shell sands of home;
but all I find is dust and tainted air,
gunpowder smell, and endless, endless slate –
no space for machair flowers, no skylark song.

*machair = the fertile sandy plain on the landward side of dunes in the west of Scotland, renowned for the variety and abundance of its wild flowers*

# Leaving Belnahua, 1914

*If the population remained the same as in the 1911 Census there would have been eight women left on the island. Mary McKay with sons Neil, Peter, Archibald, John and daughter Jeannie; Katie Black with sons Allan, Duncan and Donald; Anne McTaggart with daughters Betty and Colina; Janet Ferguson with daughter Jeannie; Mary McColl with daughter Jeannie and son Donald; and, without children, Christine McIntyre, Maggie McColl and Margaret McKay.*

After the men had gone
the island changed
sounds of their presence stilled –
warning shouts, last blast,
explosions rumbling aftermath
that shook the land
as thunder shook the sky,
metal breaking slate,
trudge of hob-nailed boots,
roll of wagon wheels,
voices harsh with dust,
even the staunch farewell
became a memory.

Still the pump went on,
its day-long-night-long thudding
marking time
as we worked shifts
to haul the coal,
keep the fire alight,
rake out the ashes,
wait for war to end –
our men's return.

Time passed –
faith in a future here
had ebbed away.
We had to leave,
life on this barren rock
too hard to thole,
our meagre bundles tied
we stopped the pump,
and in that moment
Belnahua died.

Stunned by the sudden silence,
even the children paused
as though bewitched.

Afraid to break the spell
we voiced our thoughts in whispers
became aware of sounds
we'd never heard,
small waves, a passing bird,
a light breeze combing grass.

We turned away, boarded the boat,

did not look back.

Census, 1921

No hand to sign a name.
          No occupation to record.
                    No wives. No widows.
                              Not a pauper left.

No children
          playing on the shore.
                    No mothers calling out
                              the last few names.

Nothing to stop
          the gradual decay,
                    wild things moving in,
                              the spread of grass.


          Belnahua left to wind and sea.

## Angus Shaw, 1937

*They took me back*
*but nothing was the same.*

The quarry, raped of slate
was water filled,
winding gear
lay rotting where it fell,
the shop stood empty
save for rusting scales.
its door, loose hung
was banging in the wind,
books lay mouldering
on the school room shelves,
homes deserted,
footpaths overgrown

*as if a plague had wiped*
*the people out.*

## Divers

Once divers braved the depths
found ghostly shapes half-lost
in ghostly gloom.

Trucks slate-laden,
waiting to be moved,
winding gear that tumbled from above,

pipes and pumps,
a heap of rusting bolts, the cage
that lowered men daily to their work.

Tools that wait
the hands that never come.

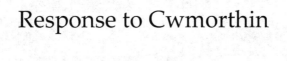

Response to Cwmorthin

the padlocked mine

## The Scale is Staggering

All day I walk on slate,
think on the Isles of Netherlorn,
how Cwmorthin's heaps and screes
would bury Belnahua,
cover Easdale's whinstone ridge;
how even Seil and Luing
would disappear,
and spoil would slip from hilltops
to the sea, rise above waves,
create new islands
            out of broken rock.

All day I walk on slate,
up to former summits
topped by waste,
grunt of raven, strident cry of chough;
past tunnels cut through rock,
the padlocked mine,
caverns, quarry floors,
broken-bouldered cliffs,
chutes of shattered scree,
land turned inside out,
            mountain heart laid bare.

All day I walk on slate,
down inclines
to the valley deep in shade,
chapel of tumbled stone, rotting wood,
rafters fallen like faith;
eerie silence fills the leaden lake,
barracks bleak-and-barren shells,
shuttered cottage, space between trees.
As I leave, a blackbird breaks to song –
slate-face echoes answer
            answer   answer   answer ...

# Slate Voices:
# Cwmorthin

# Jan Fortune

INDEPENDENT INNOVATIVE INTERNATIONAL

Published by Cinnamon Press
Meirion House
Glan yr afon
Tanygrisiau
Blaenau Ffestiniog
Gwynedd LL41 3SU
www.cinnamonpress.com

The right of Jan Fortune and Cottia Fortune-Wood to be identified as author and artist of this work has been asserted by them in accordance with the Copyright, Designs and Patent Act, 1988. © 2014
ISBN 978-1-909077-24-9

British Library Cataloguing in Publication Data. A CIP record for this book can be obtained from the British Library

Designed and typeset in Palatino by Cinnamon Press
Cover image: © Cottia Fortune-Wood
Cover design by Cottia Fortune-Wood and Jan Fortune

Printed in Poland

Cinnamon Press is represented in the UK by Inpress Ltd www.inpressbooks.co.uk and in Wales by the Welsh Books Council www.cllc.org.uk.

# Acknowledgements

Some of the poems have been previously published. An earlier version of 'Return to Tŷ Meirion' appeared in *The Lie of the Land*, Jan Fortune (ed), Cinnamon Press, (2006); 'Part 6: A Litany for Cwmorthin' appeared in *Scintilla 17: the Journal of the Vaughan Association*, February 2014; 'Tŷ Schrödinger 1' and '$C_{17}H_{19}NO_3$' were first published in *This Line Is Not For Turning*, Jane Monson (ed), Cinnamon Press, (2011).

Thanks to 'Cofio Cwmorthin Remembered', an informal community dedicated to cataloguing the social and archeological history of Cwmorthin, who kindly gave permission for the use of their archive which provided the found material for section 3 of the sequence 'Cofio — Voices from Cwmorthin'.
The following publications provided a wealth of information:
*Cwmorthin Slate Quarry*, Graham Isherwood, Adit Publications, 1995.
*Gwynedd Inheriting a Revolution*, David Gwyn, Phillimore, 2006.
*The Archaeology of Gwynedd Slate: flesh on the bones*, Michael Lewis, Snowdonia National Park, 2011
*The North Wales Quarrymen*, 1874-1922, R Merfyn Jones, University of Wales Press, 1981.

Many people have assisted in the journey of this book. Thanks to Ann Drysdale for her meticulous copy editing and to Pete Marshall for sharing a love of slate and for opportunities to read the work in progress at Ty'n y Coed. Particular thanks to my family for being encouraging, wonderful people and especially to Cottia for the powerful photography accompanying the poetry. Huge thanks to Mavis Gulliver, my co-poet, who has shared multiple drafts along the way, introduced me to the beautiful slate islands and ensured that the final book is more than the sum of its two parts.

# Contents

Anhraethol – What Cannot be Said

A Litany for Cwmorthin

Faint Order

Visiting the Islands of Netherlorn

In memory of Cwmorthin –

lives calling for narrative.

# Cwmorthin

We come over the lip

# I. Tŷ Schrödinger

the path to the chapel is long

## i. Cwm

We come over the lip, drop to the bowl where lake seeps from itself, heather underfoot, a monkey-puzzle tree beside the house. Lichen enamels walls that close round memories, dust. No one speaks. The water can't recall the smell of sweat, the taste of blood, the words for slate—the path to the chapel is long.

## ii: Slate I

Water sucks colour from sky, staccatos shore,
greys granite remains, grinds scree-scraped rock;
falls—
slate needles on lake—
the last remaining roof-tiles stutter—

It's late,

's late

slate

## iii. Home is...

on this hill, moss underfoot, heather flecking grass, hoar breath over ice. Lakeside slate forgets the shape of barracks thick with lamb fat, sugared tea, bodies slick with sweat and slate; hums of kettle, hob-nails, stone, debate; a snatch of fiery hymn that's taken up to ring off granite walls; can't imagine nights of box-bed bunks, narrow as chapel, lumpen as earth, bedding soiled with slate; how they housed the one soft thing: the barracks cat beside the range.

Ruins cannot recall who lived in the house, planted the tree: Evans, Hughes, Davies, Jones? Griffith, Gethin, Gerraint, Gwen? Owain and Blod? Ossian and Nest? Ruins will not say if those forgotten stood on this hill, wondered what would happen next.

## iv. Slaughterhouse

Beneath lake, barracks, flue, the Slaughterhouse. Old Vein, a mess of scree. Back Vein, a clutter of rusted carts, crumbling steps, iron-encrusted ropes. Ledges drop to chambers, flooded now. There are no bargain gangs — rockman, splitter, dresser — haggling pay, talked down by slate-eyed setting stewards who look to managers that speak no Welsh. A *bargain* when the rock is bad, when after paying for ropes, chains, candle stubs, for sharpening tools, there's nothing left. A *bargain* when to make a wage means robbing pillars holding back cathedra-chamber weight; splitting rocks that hold the mountains overhead, till beveled columns sag; bring the darkness down.

## v. Queen Mary Cafe

Beside the door, a shelf; two shovels rust, the dust of ghosts who gathered once to eat here, speak in formal tones of Disestablishment or politics, hold Eisteddfoddau or practise hymns, while one kept minutes by a candle's light, as though these lives were worth remembering. Above the door, the caban's name: for one who burned dissenters such as these.

## vi. Cail

No hymns. Windows croon the strain of wind. Archways reach towards a glowering sky. No roof. No children chanting numbers, letters. No longer schoolhouse, chapel. *Cail*: the Sheepfold shelters animals now. Once these stones sang to praise a lamb slaughtered for their sake — *cigiddio*. No hymns. The moan of wind cries *marw* for the slaughtered; *marw, marw* through the broken arch.

## vii. Corpse Candles

hover pale and low: white —a woman, red — a man, faint — a child;
warn of death that night. Two lights bring double sorrow to a single
home. How many brooded over the face of the lake the eve of the Great
Fall? Did heather glimmer red? Did no one see the warning lights, pale
and slow, before their candles dimmed?

## viii. Cwmcerthin

Cwmorthin: from *Cwm-certh-hin:*
cwm for valley;
    -certh for awful/dangerous;
        -hin for weather.
Darkness on the face of the earth,
        a litany of awfulness:
    Mae hi'n bwrw glaw,
           *it rains*
    mae hi'n cesair,
           *it hails,*
    mae hi'n eira.
           *it snows.*
    Mae hi'n arllwys.
           *It's pouring down.*
    Mae hi'n chwerw ac ddiflas.
           *It's bitter and miserable.*
    Mae hi'n mellt a tharanau.
           *It's thundering and lightning.*
    Mae hi'n ofnadwy.
           *It's terrible.*
    Mae hi'n tywyll.
           *It's dark—*
           over the face of the deep —
Cwmorthin: from *Cwm-certh-hin:.*

## ix. Slaughterhouse II

What brings the darkness down? A slip of foot across the precipice; a wagon breaking links to run amok; a rock that tumbles splitting one man's skull; a labourer who startles at a shout; a carpenter who cartwheels from a bridge; a severed chain that hurls a rockman down; a fall of chamber roof; a slab that's blasted free; a mis-step on a bridge; the movement of a baulk before the drop; the prising of a roof that slams to ground; a hidden joint that spews its block of slate, the crushed man lingering on for sixteen days; an always unexpected fall of rock; a handle on a crane that crushes skull; a handle spinning wildly into bone; an avalanche of stone while clearing fall; a winch that screams to flail out of control; a slab descending in advance of blast; a wagon striking rock; a roof-fall

$$-all \ will \ bring \ the \ darkness \ down.$$

## x. Merch

So many tales and none. Ffestiniog wives are talked of: marry young, do not know thrift or cooking skills, serve pancakes butter-soaked. Children raising children play at house; must have their toys: eight guinea clocks, large as Goliath's coffin; cabinets of china dogs, pianos, crockery; spend what husbands earn on frippery while men go comfortless, cannot turn for trinkets strewn through sanctuaries. Parlours are for show, not places tired men can sit. But what else should they do, these girls, but gossip, preen and breed their lives away?

So many tales and none in our voice, told by mine inspectors, doctors, novelists who paint us lazy and extravagant, by ladies condescending to instruct 'the poor' with cooking skills. And those of us far flung whose husbands walk to work, five miles on mountain paths, who keep faith with this unforgiving land; and those at Rhosydd Terrace by the Chapel, what do you know of us? That we lived and died as though we'd never been?

## xi. Slate II

I come here seeking stillness. The sounds are not of hewing, hacking, hosing-down, but lapping lake and restless wind. No one rives slate raw; splitting slabs to wafer thins along the grain. Beneath the rocks, the Slaughterhouse is empty now of all but rusting carts, ladders, tracks; tunnels layered with ghosts whose mallets, chisels dull like candle stubs.

## xii. We come here

when sun stalls, snagged in clouds. Water lapping shore as yesterday, as for a million years. We stand below beams that sigh a weight of snow; sag onto slabs, stone—the shape of refuge hollowed out: roof-slates gone, a splintered floor. Between gale's moans, the scrape of iron ghosts, graunch of metal, blacksmith's clang, hacking, hewing, hosing-down; rock-dust coughs that mined their lungs to death. Winds whine hymns that haunt the Sheepfold still, its roof open to hail.
                                        We hunch.
                                        Hug walls against the cold.
*Shush*, you say.

## xiii. Tŷ Schrödinger I

The one remaining house is closed: windows boarded, padlocks guard the doors. Inside, unseen inhabitants, their lives already past, are yet alive and dead—until the seal gives way to break the spell. We know that they are gone, the dead, not smeared into some living-dying-life-inside-the-box; not caught between—but do not know the how or when the murk of maybes became death.
And in our box we wait until the measurement is made.

## xiv. Clwt

Braced for wind – black teeth of slate on rusted wire. Between the barbs, a faded rag, ferrous stained. Did she feel the fabric catch? Did he slip from barracks to meet her there? Did he try to set her free?
In February storm, my purple between the slabs of mudstone crushed to slate: the space between a woman and a man.

## xv. Tŷ Schrödinger II

*The distinction between past, present, and future is only a...persistent illusion*
Einstein

After snow rends beams; rain peels paint, pulps wood; frost splits tiles — the house has sagged. Yet, if future, present, past are blurred, perhaps a hundred years from here they feel the drip of rain through roof, look out on snow around our lake, glimpse the couple we could have been before the roof gave way.

## xvi. Depths

*A lake is the landscape's most beautiful and expressive feature. It is earth's eye, looking into which the beholder measures the depths of his own nature.*
Henry David Thoreau, Walden

Around the shore, peaks take stock, measure height and width, outcrops poised to shear, boulders slicing lines, the way a tree tilts down to shale-sharp earth, the rucks and shadows of each face. The mirror shows it all: decaying barracks huddled in the snow, the gap-toothed fence of slate, the remnants caught on barbs, the first tile missing from Tŷ Schrödinger—

and all the empty spaces in between...

# II. A Glossary for Cwmorthin

those who have gone

# Bilingual Alphabet

A is for adit, the entrance that waits
B is for bad rock — vast useless tons —
for barracks, black powder to blast away slate,
B for the blocks that we bargain for pay.
C is for chamber, cathedrals to work
C is for candles, our only dim light,
for cupboarding — cutting the pillars away,
And C is for caban, to eat, think, debate.
Ch is for chwarel, the quarry we work.
D is for drum for winding the ropes.
Dd is for ddoe, when the last day mutates.
E is for English, a foreigner's tongue.
E is for eira when the snows come.
F for fire-setting to loosen the slate,
F for the floor, for the level we work.
Ff for Ffestiniog valley that's home.
G is for gang, in whom we trust,
And G is for gas that stifles our breath.
H is for hunter, large circular saw.
I is for iaith, the language we live.
J is for jwmpah, though none yn Gymraeg,
the long weighted rod that bores into rock.
K is a letter that doesn't live here.
L is for launder, the deep water-trough,
Ll is for llechi, for slate and for llyn.
M is for mill where blocks are reduced.
Ng for mutations, dream of fy ngardd
P is for pillar to stave off the fall
P for the powder house, explosives store.
Ph is for cough; an aspirate mutate,
peswch to pheswch, always too late.
R is for rubbish, the vast tons of waste.
Rh is for rhys, large mallet for blocks
S for the slideway to push the blocks down
And S is for strike, tunnelling vein.
T is for trimmer to size roofing slates,
T is for twll, the pit that we mine.
Th is for middles: as 'methu', mistake —
for what we can't speak of, anhraethol.
U for untopping, moves rock from above.
V is for nothing here yn Gymraeg.
W — waliau, sheds where slate's dressed,

And for the winding house, sheltering drum.
Nothing is X and nothing is Z,
but Y is for yma, for here in this place;
for ymadawedig, those who have gone.

*Ymadawedig = departed; Anhraethol = unspeakable; Methu – falter – a mistake; Peswch = cough; Llyn = lake; llechi + slate; Ddoe yesterday; Fy ngarrd = my garden*

# III. Cofio — Voices from Cwmorthin

This land is…

*Hidden above steps, this deep valley has long been a place of hardship, remote living and industry. Deserted now, it was once home to many — farmers who came in the twelfth century; nineteenth century miners, gathered in the slate boom years, pausing for the First World War, mining into the 40s, when the mining dwindled until only ghosts remained.*

## i. Contested Histories

a. *Peniarth Papers collection, National Library of Wales [ref: DA33].*

It starts in 1541, the challenge ringing:
  *Let it be known*
    The legalese of names, phrases, dates:
Ieuan ap Gruffudd ap John
    Free Tennant of the King
      The Court of Chancery, 1556 to 58,
The case between
    William ap Ieuan, alias Jevans,
      *A pore prentice in the city of London*
        His brother John,
        *Cumorthyn*
          *Land in the township of Ffestiniog.*
Poor William won:
  *This land is my land*
    William Evans, now of Slaugham, Sussex, clerk,
      *My land, not to live, but lease:*
        November, year of our Lord, 1608
        to one Evan Lloyd, Penmachno.

*b. However in the Caerynwch collection held at the National Library of Wales, a letter dated December 7th 1838 from William Ormsby-Gore of Porkington (now Brogyntyn) to a W P Richards of London, gives a conflicting picture.*

*This land's not your land*
    *This land is my land*
Examine the deeds:
    Cwmorthin Ucha, Brogyntyn Estate, held by me
See that Queen Elizabeth granted letters – 1577 –
    Robert Dudley, Earl of Leicester
The date is clear:
    11th July,
        22nd July,
            31st July (1578.)
Succession is clear:
    On Dudley's death to the Earl of Warwick –
        To Lady Ann, Countess of Warwick –
            Sold to Lord St. John of …
                Who sold to Leonard Baker, 1595.
Letters suggest the mortgage was not paid,
    control passed to Sir William Maurice, Clenennau,
        eldest of eight known children
*Land to the eldest; land to the legitimate*
    descended from a line of men
        holding office in North Wales.
*Land to the strong.*
    *This land is my land.*

This land is William's land
    Wives: Margaret – Ellin – Jane
        Children: nine by Margaret – one by Ellin
Sheriff (twice): Caernarvonshire 1593 – Beaumaris 1601
    Debated tirelessly
        Staunch Anglican and Royalist
*This land is their land.*
    Knighted 1603
        Lies in Penmorfa church

## ii. Tenants

*The Henry Rumsey Williams papers add further confusion to the question of ownership. At various dates the lands are mentioned with reference to a Richard Owen Esq and his wife Elizabeth (1710); the Rt Hon Richard Lord Bulkeley and Lady Jane Bulkeley (1741); Edward Williams and Lady Jane (1767) and Jane Williams, eldest daughter of Edward and Lady Jane. There is also a sale in 1799 to William Wynne of Pennarth.*

*Rent books of the Brogyntyn Estate catalogue:*

*This land is absent landlord land*
A litany of lease and rising rents
1727 Cwmorthin Ucha
    £8 per year
        tenant William Pritchard
Cwmorthin Issa
    the lesser sum, £6 per year
        Robert Humphreys
            passed to Humphreys, Anne, 1744
                to Cadwallader, Owen, 1766
                  £10 annually
                    £18 in 1774
                        to £26 by 1788.

Pritchard rented Ucha till 1773
    passed to one John Williams
        annual rent £12
            £13 4s by 1794
                (including rent of Tanygrisiau Farm)
                    held to 1804 – rate unchanged
*This land is confiscated land*
    1782: A writ of George III
        William Wynne – Pennarth – outlawed.
A list of properties seized:
    mills
        a fishery
            several hundred acres in Tanygrisiau and Ffestiniog
                a farm — Cwm hirthin Issa.

1861, July:
      Cwm-Orthin Slate Company
          bought the freehold of Cwmorthin.
The farm was occupied
      until buried by waste.
*This land is worked land*
      *This land is their land.*

## iii. Visitors

### a. 1781

*In his* Tour in Wales, *Pennant records that Cwmorthin was difficult to access.*

About a mile from Cynfael,
the Pengwern Arms
received me often after arduous trips.
Opposite lies Cwmorthin;
more hidden, more difficult to reach
than even Cwmbychan.
I first descended into woods,
the road was steep,
the valley narrow, ascent was hazardous.
I grew fatigued
on dangerous paths; rock-strewn, slight,
up mountain ways
attempted rarely, I believe, by horse.

### b. 1875

*In* Cymru (A National Dictionary of Wales) *Owen Jones gives an account of descent from the Cwm:*

The road lies on a hill above the Cwm,
or rather, roads remains,
an ancient way from Cricieth to Llanrwst.
Britons of old preferred to make roads high,
avoiding animals that roamed below.

A remote path from Cwmorthin
where grisiau of sorts – steps – near Tai y Muriau –
descended to Dol Rhedyn, known as Grisiau Mawr.
And on account of these 'great steps' the area below
was known as Tan y grisiau —
Beneath the Steps.


c. 1882

*In Hanes Plwyf Festiniog GJ Williams wrote that in the absence of a road from Tanygrisiau:*

The only way was through Cwmorthin.
Steps were climbed.
The slope difficult with an animal.

I recalled the Reverend Freeman,
*Sketches in Wales,*
amazed to see a tenant negotiate the place on horse.

Like Owen Jones we entered from north-west,
set up a pile of slates,
memorial to our visit, before departing for Cwmorthin.

The first part of our way was over broad morass –
of heather, peat,
before most horrible descent – crags like nature's ruins.

In the dreary bottom in the gloomy dark
a lake of some extent
surrounded on all sides by sheer and rocky hills.

On its shores half a dozen patches of potatoes, oats
and, at the lower end,
a house smothered in rocks — where I did not see a living thing.

Nearby, two or three enclosures cleared of stone,
producing herbage.
Cascades tumbled from the circumambient cliffs

to feed a pool disgorging in a torrent.
This Cwm and lake,
enclosed by mountains rising to a lofty altitude.

Surely, never was any spot more gloomy and remote.
Daylight and productiveness
must be for more than half the year excluded.

Descent, the most extraordinary I have made,
was burdensome.
It was a chain of steps — winding crags down stairs.

Beside the steps, the river issues from the llyn above,
forms waterfalls,
pours one sheet over ledges of rock or scatters them

with infinite division, hiding its secret tide
among hollows,
fissures, where it roars unseen.

Half way down we met a farmer, and sure-footed mare,
climbing to his tenement
and he descended to a nook in rocks to let us pass,

which I presumed amongst his better
mowing fields
for here was vegetation – rushes, flags.

And I was much amused to observe the painful movement
of himself and beast
progressing up these rocky, miserable stairs.


## iv. Join the Union

Strong at Dinorwic, Penrhyn, yet not at Oakley where,
of sixteen hundred men, two hundred only join the cause,
but here, remote, with not three hundred men, six in ten are ours,
who won't be bought
                    by charity,
                              allowances
                                        or profit schemes,
who'll all down tools when called.

## v. The Underground Men, 1936

They stand or sit on slate, rockmen, miners, labourers,
dust-laden, grinning at the lens, flanked by steward,
haulier with horse.
They stand:
Jones, Lewis, Jones, Morris, Owen, Evans, Edwards, Owen,
Thomas, Jones, Jones, Roberts, Williams, horse;
crouch:
Hughes, Thomas, Roberts, Jones, Thomas, Owen, Davies, Jones;
sit like school-boys:
Jones, Jones, Hughes, Hughes, Davies.

Their names people this valley still.
The work has long since gone.


## vi. This Land is For Sale

*1948 — catalogue pages from the auction of Cwmorthin Uchaf by the Brogyntyn
Estate. The agent, Peter Jenkins of Brecon, says:*

My Great Uncle Sydney, Captain Matthews,
bought all the lots in Ffestiniog
sold a chunk to MANWEB for the Stwlan Hydro Scheme,
acquired the mineral rights on Park and Croesor,
Clough Williams Ellis bought the surface,
and later mineral rights on all but land round Croesor,
where ICI kept an explosives store.

Captain Matthews' daughters were Pauline and Gwynneth.
Gwynneth died last year. Pauline is in excellent fettle.
Both unmarried, first cousins of my mother,
my son, Tim, is Pauline's cousin, twice removed –
given the land before he left for Australia;
the best man to solve problems like the Reservoirs Act.

*This land is his land.*
Tim has freehold – 870 acres or thereabouts –
around Cwmorthin, Cwmorthin Uchaf too,
a lozenge on the map.

lakeside slate forgets the shape of barracks

# IV. Nursery Rhymes for Cwmorthin

dry your tears, forget the blood

## Weeping Song

Hush! Hush! The slates do crush
The pillars are falling down
Death to claim
Others to maim
Till weeping's heard in town.


## If All Our Veins

If all the hills were empty,
And all the lakes were milk,
If all the trees were bread and cheese,
Would we be dressed in silk?

If all our veins were sturdy,
If none but had a crack,
If all the chambers shone with light
Would any break his back?

## The Bad Rockman's Song

If I'd as much money as I could say
I never would carry bad rock away
Bad rock away, a ton till pay,
I never would carry bad rock away.

If I'd as much money as I could tell,
I'd never clear rock from the face of hell,
The face of hell, slate dust and smell,
I'd never clear rock from the face of hell.

## Catwalking

Catwalk-stealthy rockman
Climbed the wall of slate,
With only a candle,
a rope to ward off fate,

Down came the rockfall,
Down came the rain.
Will catwalk-stealthy rockman
climb the slate again?

# The Slate Dresser's Rhyme

This slate dresser, he made one,
He made Empress good and strong —
With a dry your tears, forget the blood,
Jump over the moon and down to the lake.

This slate dresser he made two,
Princess, Duchess straight and true —
With a *Sych dy lygaid, anghofia'r gwaed,*
*Naid dros y lleuad ac i lawr at y llyn.*

This slate dresser, he made three,
Small Duchess, Marchioness, Countess Broad — see —
With a dry your tears, forget the blood,
Jump over the moon and down to the lake.

This slate dresser, he made four,
the countess trio, wide lady for the door —
With a *Sych dy lygaid, anghofia'r gwaed,*
*Naid dros y lleuad ac i lawr at y llyn.*

This slate dresser he made five,
Two ladies, two headers, small lady rived —
With a dry your tears, forget the blood,
Jump over the moon and down to the lake.

This slate dresser, he made six
lady, header, two Doubles, two Singles to fix —
With a *Sych dy lygaid, anghofia'r gwaed,*
*Naid dros y lleuad ac i lawr at y llyn.*

*Welsh lines from Gee cefyl bach (Gee up, little horse) traditional*

# Lullaby

*Cysga di fy mhlentyn tlws*
*Cei gysgu tan y bore*

O I wish your dad was home with us
Not barracked in the damp
I wish your dad worked in the sun
Not by a candle lamp.

Go to sleep my pretty baby,
You can sleep till morning.

O I wish your brother went to school
Not into chambers cold
For your brother is a *rybelwr*
And soon he will grow old

*Cysga di fy mhlentyn tlws*
*Cei gysgu tan y bore*

O I wish they dined off mutton stew
Not thick sweet tea and bread
O I wish I did not hear the cough
I've heard from men now dead.

Go to sleep my pretty baby,
You can sleep till morning.

*Cysga di fy mhlentyn tlws*
*Cei gysgu tan y bore*

Go to sleep my pretty baby,
You can sleep till morning.

*Traditional – Cysga di, go to sleep*

# V. Anhraethol - What Cannot be Said

walk up against rules – crunch boots on rubble

## i. Cwmorthin for two voices

And the snow falls and falls
on the greying face of slate
and the ruined village calls                    And the snow falls

through crumbling granite walls          and falls
through the river's crashing spate
and as snow falls and falls                      and the ruined village calls

the wind keens and crawls
into crevices to wait,
still the ruined village calls                    as the snow falls

as a hush of ice-web palls                      and falls
buries broken barn and gate
while the snow falls and falls                and the ruined village calls

on the mill's shattered halls
slipping to a silent fate,
and the ruined village calls                    as the snow falls

out its grief as it falls                             and falls
and it knows it is too late
and the snow falls and falls                    and the ruined village calls
and the ruined village calls                    as the snow falls
                                                              and falls

## ii. Slaughterhouse III

brings    dark-
                ness  down—
slip   foot        prec-
                   ip-
                     ice
wagon     break
              ing   links
rock       tum
             bles   splitting sk-
                        ull
startles    falls     unfenced
                       c
               s      a
              l         r
              e         t
               e     w
                 h
sev     ered   chain
             hurls
                d
             o
            w
             n
           fall
   chamber roof
            slab    blasted
         free          miss-step
  drop   roof           slams  to
            ground
spews     block      crushed man ling-
                           ers…
unexpected
         f
       a
      l
      l

crane    crushes       skull
        bone    ava-
                    lanche
winch              out of       con-
                                  trol
slab    blast    striking       rock
        roof-
            fall —
                brings    darkness
                              d
                        o
                          w
                            n.

## iii. Vanishing Trick

lake      laps
             rubble
nibbles
      rock
         grain
         by
         grain
r     a     i    n
              fingers granite,
                  softens slates,
the strangle-kiss     of moss,
l
o
n
g-t
  a
    l
     l
    o
      n
       e
      d    damp's
            exquisite reach,
decay gnaws,
       freezes,
          cracks,
            bends,
              breaks,
how    ap
    h   e
    c    l
      becomes
         s   h   e
        d       e
        l       p
          o   f
barracks
     b   r    a
       e    k

how the last house
                    slips
                        a sl-
                            a-
                            te,
gives in to vanishing
how a world
                ebbs
in a baptism of  r      i
                    a     n
ends
in r   u    n
            i
by a shushing lake,
buried
        in this c     m
                    w
so silent
        that to speak's as though
                already
                    talking
                            to the dead.


## iv. Shrive

grasses on the shore,
buds between boulders,
unbearable hope of spring --

## v. Incline

*In an 1895 Parliamentary Mines Enquiry, a witness spoke of the lack of paths*
*underground for men to go to their work, forcing them to use the inclines, which were*
*in use by wagons and machinery.*

walk up
  against rules —
          steam


        candle — flickers
              blocks falling
              up — walk incline


                    pipes hiss
                        steam —
                  candle guttters


                            no light —
                                steam
                                    hiss


                                crunch
                                    boots
                              on rubble --


                          bones
                        crack the
                        silence


                    before wagon —
                  no warning
              cover


              too far —
                  candle
                      doused.

# VI. A Litany for Cwmorthin

memory so close the stones might shout

## i. Called

A single roof-beam, soaked —
rain, hymns,
stutter of wind:

> *But the Lord was not in the wind.*

Once mountains quaked
to blast and hammer:

> *But the Lord was not in the quake.*

Dust choked the clouds,
smoke from barracks, mills:

> *But the Lord was not in the fire.*

Memory so close the stones
might shout

> *But the Lord was not...*

## ii. Ashes

A stilted March of snow and thaw and snow,
white sky, white mountain,
ice-melt scorching tongues,
the buried land.

*remember one day you will die.*

Echoes slow as slate:

*Answer me when I call*
*Answer me when*
*Answer me*
*Answer*

wind against rock

*I cry to you by day*

the chanting of rain,

*remember one day you will die*

echoes slow as slate

*return to the dust of the earth*


## iii. Vigil

Wind desiccates tongues,

*stay with me*

slate dust chokes,

*watch with me*

we wait –

*pray with me*

What can we pray?

*Have mercy?*

Wind speaks in tongues

*Eleison*
*Eleison*
*Eleison*

Is silent now

*just say the word*

But no Word comes.

## iv. Saturday

the empty cwm,
field frozen,
clock ticks,
slows
   to almost
     stop.

Daylight shelters
ghosts—
   shadows
   on rock.

## v. Hallelujah

Long past Imbolc,
beneath a stick-thin tree:
a single snowdrop.

Daylight shelters ghosts

# VII. Faint Order

*Trust me, this will take time, but there is order here, very faint, very human.*
Michael Ondaatje, In the Skin of a Lion

how the long dead called me here

## i. Metamorphic I

Mudstone to slate, flowers to owl,
we live with alchemy in this place.

Cwmorthin slate for a Roman fort, Tomen y Mur,
transforming the place of Blodeuwedd and Llue.

Flowers for a girl to make him a bride.
Primrose, nettle and broom.

Mudstone to slate, flowers to owl.
Cockle and bean, meadow-sweet, oak.

Mudstone to slate, flowers to owl.
Chestnut and thorn. She wants to be flowers.

Mudstone to slate, flowers to owl.
Flowers for a face, fair dexterous one.

She wants to be flowers;
                              they make her an owl —

*y gofod rhwng merch a ddyn* —
                              the space between woman and man —

Mudstone to slate.
Flowers to owl.

She wants to be...

## ii. I return

to the house,
lake lapping the door,
the day we walked
in thickening snow,
how I imagined rebuilding –
shelves for books;
upstairs, a bed –
for one.

We walked till twilight,
turned for home,
other memories,
scree under ice;
mountain to left,
river to right
and the boys —
                    descending,
                              ahead.

## iii. Cail II

Once I watched a dying man
play hymns for his own requiem,

intoned the names of the dead --
heaped carnations on an altar cloth --

lifted cup and bread
as if in memory,

left candles flickering
when the lights went out,

and walked with coffins
to the tolling bell.

Yet only in this roofless *cail*,
hunched against the rain

have I thought that resurrection might be close,
believed: *it's not too late,*

failed to see the roof already gone,
arches broken, ruin in the walls,

failed to hear the silence
after wind.

## iv. $C_{17}H_{19}NO_3$

You are right. When I picture him it is not the glint of eyes or the slow curl of his mouth, but the length of his body huddled into the coarse stuff of an ancient jacket; the scuffed brown boots scarred from descending scree. How he planted a track.

You are right. And yet I can't help thinking the air has taken a cold metallic taste.

Morpheus, god of dreams, son of Hypnos, god of sleep. I know its shape, its bonds, its formula. I know how it changes the light like snow; how it numbs the senses, reduces pain, induces sleep. I know how morphine lies; like snow.

When I think of him I think of snow on Cwmorthin ruins: the sight of his retreating back, his footsteps harder to follow, even when he was still; how I watched his slow retreat as though he would melt.

## v. Tŷ Schrödinger III

I am divided up in time, whose order I do not know, and my thoughts are torn with every kind of tumult.

Augustine, Confessions

*for Omar*

You say, mystery makes sacrament,
that my closed door is proof against profane,
but today the roof has split;
snow and ice gnaw tiles,
splinter slates,
the door is rupturing.

I can't see in,
wonder if those lives, unseen,
ever existed at all.

We cannot write of death.
Approach only to find soul
broken by memory,
slice of a moment
in which we taste –
exile, return –

an ecstasy
already
     not yet

## vii. Tŷ Schrödinger IV

*We tell stories because in the last analysis human lives need and merit being narrated...*
*The whole history of suffering cries out for vengeance and calls for narrative.*
Paul Ricoeur, Time and Narrative, Volume 1

How this place honours ghosts,
how the long dead called me here
how mill house, engine, slate dust, noise
– are gone;
         how rain spears stone,

Tŷ Schrödinger is empty now,
an exodus Beneath the Steps,
abandoned homes.

How I came here
trailing broken wings,
shoulders rigid as faith;
how I healed
         and broke,

came to Cwmorthin in snow,
longed for this house
in its fold of slate.

How you left.

How Tŷ Schrödinger cracked –
the weight of years on stone
              let go.

## viii. Cail III

And I will go in peace without a prayer,
gather flowers -- nettle and broom,
carry tokens -- feather and slate,
I will walk from this cwm,
remember the ghosts
who called me here.

## ix. Year's Turn Beneath the Steps

World drained to grey,
a phosphorous lamp,
one clod of snow.

Beyond the fence, mountains,
wind, the sag of marsh,
a hiss of stream.

A firework rips
the night.  We lean
towards New Year.

## x. Return to Tŷ Meirion

I want a house – secluded,
a place to keep the chaos
out, a granite womb:
slung against slate,
hills; the sound of birds
hurtling to stake their claims,
while wind intones its lullaby.

We become so used
to fractured days,
to weeks spent
keeping one step
ahead of the rains;

to months when all we can do
is mend the fence,
then mend the fence,
then mend the fence;

to endless years when
it is enough
to name the things
that anchor us –

this photograph
of a younger face,

this picture book
that I read to them

a thousand times,
this yellow shell,

this scrap of slate.

I want this place –
a foot on the crumbling earth.

# Visiting the Islands of Netherlorn

a netherworld – far out, slung low

## From Slate to Slate

Tossed into sea and sky –
a netherworld – far out, slung low,
a place on edge as Blaenau is,
Netherlorn – bereft of industry,
of noise of blast of boom
of pounding pumps,
the rhythmic clattering of slates:
Skalzi
      Llechi
            Skalzi
                  Slate

In place of shouts, the sush of waves,
the hurl of wind,
the shrill of gulls,
the blackbirds warning call,
the names of things
that grow on
Skalzi
      Llechi
            Skalzi
                  Slate


lichen coltsfoot celandine
blackthorn primrose gorse
nettle daisy heather moss
scurvy grass and buckler fern
great hairy woodrush rose
yarrow foxglove thale cress
earth-nut bramble plantain
ragwort ivy eyebright thyme,
and on the beach the slate-flake-sand
silver tommies seaglass periwinkle shells
Skalzi
      Llechi
            Skalzi
                  Slate